I AM NOT A TOILET ROLL

THE RECYCLING PROJECT BOOK

THIS IS A CARLTON BOOK

Published in 2018 by Carlton Books Limited, an imprint of the
Carlton Publishing Group, 20 Mortimer Street, London W1T 3JW

A catalogue record for this book is available from the British Library.

ISBN: 978-1-78312-406-0

Printed in Dongguan, China

10 9 8 7 6 5 4 3 2 1

Author: Sara Stanford
Creative Director: Clare Baggaley
Written, designed, illustrated and packaged by: Dynamo Limited
Senior Production Controller: Yael Steinitz
Design Manager: Emily Clarke
Executive Editor: Stephanie Stahl
Publisher: Russell McLean

I AM NOT A TOILET ROLL

THE RECYCLING PROJECT BOOK

CARLTON KIDS

INCREDIBLE THINGS TO MAKE WITH TOILET ROLLS!

Hi THERE!

ARE YOU READY TO GET MAKING? OF COURSE YOU ARE!

THIS CRAFT BOOK IS JAM-PACKED WITH RECYCLABLE ARTY PROJECTS AND SIMPLE STEP-BY-STEP GUIDES. YOU'LL FIND OUT HOW TO TURN TOILET ROLLS INTO UNICORNS, SHARKS, PIRATES AND SO MUCH MORE!

IF YOU'D LIKE, YOU CAN USE OUR HANDY CUTOUT BITS AND PIECES AT THE BACK OF YOUR BOOK TO HELP YOU WITH YOUR CRAFTS.

YOU WILL NEED

- LOTS OF TOILET ROLLS
- TAPE
- GLUE
- COLOURFUL PAPER
- COLOURFUL CARD
- PAINTS
- PAINT BRUSHES
- SAFETY SCISSORS
- STRING
- TIN FOIL
- GLITTER
- LOLLIPOP STICKS
- PENS
- PENCILS

YOU'LL NEED A GROWN-UP TO HELP YOU WITH ALL OF THE MAKES!

CONTENTS

SHAAAAARK!

I'M A **TERRIFYING** SHARK HERE TO **CHOMP** ON UNSUSPECTING **TOES** IN THE **BATHTUB!** I DEFINITELY WOULDN'T TURN TO TOILET ROLL MUSH UNDERWATER...

WATCH OUT!!

YOU WILL NEED

- ONE EMPTY TOILET ROLL
- BLUE AND WHITE PAINT
- PAINT BRUSH AND PEN
- SAFETY SCISSORS
- BLUE AND WHITE CARD
- A BOWL (TO DRAW AROUND)
- TAPE
- GOOGLY EYES

SET THE SCENE

Make your shark a perfect undersea background by tearing up strips of blue tissue paper and sticking them onto some card. Add bits of tin foil to make the water really sparkle! Use finger paints to make orange and pink coral on the sea floor. Are you ready to make this toothy toilet roll into a dangerous shark? Flip the page to find out how!

DID YOU KNOW? BABY SHARKS ARE CALLED PUPS!

GO FURTHER!

NEXT USE THESE SKILLS TO MAKE A CHOMPY ALLIGATOR. TURN OVER TO FIND OUT HOW!

I'M A SHARK!

1

Paint your toilet roll so that one half is white and the other half is blue. When the paint is completely dry, snip two triangles out of the end of the toilet roll to make the shark's mouth.

2

To make the tail, draw a circle onto the blue card by drawing around a bowl (a cereal bowl would be perfect). Then carefully cut a large triangle out of the circle, just like the above picture.

3

Roll the two sides of your blue circle together to make a cone and tape it in place. Slot the cone into the end of the toilet roll and tape it together.

4

Add extra details by cutting these tail and fin shapes from your blue card, then tape them on.

5

Create a set of pointy teeth by cutting zigzags out of two strips of white card. Stick them along the top and bottom of the shark's mouth.

6

Complete your fearsome shark by adding some googly eyes from the back of your book.

I AM NOT A TOILET ROLL...
I'M AN ALLIGATOR!

This time, paint two toilet rolls green and tape them together to make the body. Snip in a mouth shape, just like last time, and add your spiky teeth. Then, cut a pointy tail and feet from green card and stick on googly eyes. Finally, cut out green triangles of card and stick these to the alligator's back!

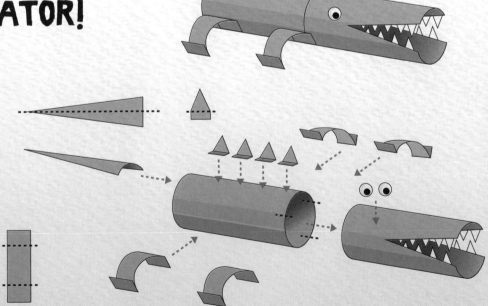

BAT!

I'M A BRILLIANT BLACK BAT, CAN'T YOU SEE?

I SLEEP DANGLING UPSIDE DOWN FROM THE VERY TALLEST OF TREES.

I ONLY COME OUT AFTER DARK, WHEN I FLAP MY BIG WINGS AND SOAR BENEATH THE STARS.

YOU WILL NEED

- ONE EMPTY TOILET ROLL
- BLACK PAINT AND A BRUSH
- TAPE AND GLUE
- BLACK AND WHITE CARD
- SAFE SCISSORS
- GOOGLY EYES

SET THE SCENE

Create a background for your bat using night-time colours – dark blue or black work best! Paint a shiny moon and stars in yellow, or cut them out using tin foil and stick them down. Add a sprinkle of glitter for shooting stars, too. Turn over to find out how to make your very own bat-tastic buddy in six easy steps!

IT'S SO COMFY SNOOZING UPSIDE DOWN. ZZZZ!

DID YOU KNOW? THERE ARE OVER 1,000 DIFFERENT TYPES OF BAT SPECIES ON THE PLANET!

GO FURTHER!

AS WELL AS A BAT, YOU CAN ALSO MAKE A FOX OR PEACOCK USING THIS TECHNIQUE. JUST TURN OVER AND WE WILL SHOW YOU HOW.

I'M A BAT!

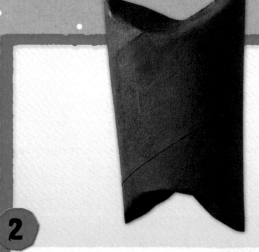

1

Fold the ends of your toilet roll towards each other to give your bat some ears. Now do the same to the bottom of your toilet roll to make the bat's feet. Tape the shape in place if needed.

2

Paint your toilet roll in your battiest black all over, then leave to dry while you do Step 3.

3

To make your bat's wings, carefully cut a big 'm' shape into black card. Snip some points along the bottom edge, like the picture, above.

4

When your painted toilet roll is dry, use a dab of glue to stick it to the middle of your wings.

5

Take a pair of googly eyes and place them towards the top of your toilet roll, under the ears.

6

Finally, give your bat some spooky fangs by cutting two small triangles out of white card. Stick them on and your bat is ready to take flight!

I AM NOT A TOILET ROLL...
I'M A FOX!

To make your fox, paint a toilet roll orange and only fold over the top of the toilet roll, not the bottom. Then, replace the bat wings with a bushy tail shape cut out from card and tape it to the back of the fox's body. For the face, snip out a white heart-shape, add googly eyes and black whiskers.

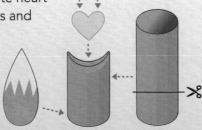

I AM NOT A TOILET ROLL...
I'M A PEACOCK!

If you can make a fox, then you can make a peacock! Look at the diagram and you will see that the same teardrop shape that is used for the fox tail can be used for peacock feathers. Also use the heart shape, but on its tummy this time!

ELEPHANT!

WITH MY **HUGE** FEET AND A 'TOOT' OF MY TRUNK, I MAKE QUITE A RACKET. NO TOILET ROLL COULD EVER BE AS NOISY AS ME!.

STOMP, STOMP, STOMP!

YOU WILL NEED

- ONE EMPTY TOILET ROLL
- WHITE, BLACK AND GREY PAINT
- PAINT BRUSH
- BLACK PEN OR PENCIL
- GLUE
- GOOGLY EYES

SET THE SCENE

Make a jungle scene for your elephant pal by layering different shades of green. You could even try making tree trunks from kitchen roll tubes painted brown. Flip the page to see how to make a rumble in the jungle by turning your toilet roll into a mighty elephant!

Flip the page to see how to make a rumble in the jungle by turning your toilet roll into a mighty elephant!

TRUMPETY TRUMP!

GO FURTHER!

YOU CAN MAKE AN EIGHT-LEGGED OCTOPUS PAL FROM A TOILET ROLL, TOO! WE'LL SHOW YOU EXACTLY WHAT TO DO ON THE NEXT PAGE.

I AM NOT A TOILET ROLL...

I'M AN ELEPHANT

1

For the trunk, make two cuts from the bottom of the toilet roll until you reach about halfway up.

2

Carefully cut big ear shapes on each side of your toilet roll (be sure to leave enough room for the elephant's face in the middle). Then, fold the ears forward to make them stick out.

3

Cut two long, thin triangles either side of the first cuts you made, leaving two tusk shapes at the top of each one. Now paint your elephant!

4

When the paint is dry, dot toenails onto the elephant's feet using the other end of the paintbrush. Add more details with a black pen.

5

Stick on some googly eyes from the back of your book to make your elephant come to life!

6

Paint a shadow onto the ears of your elephant, using black paint to add a bit of extra detail.

I AM NOT A TOILET ROLL...
I'M AN OCTOPUS!

Do you fancy making an octopus instead? Carefully snip the base of your toilet roll into eight legs – you should aim to cut about halfway up the toilet roll. Then fold down the legs, like this. Finally, paint your octopus in bright colours and leave it to dry, before adding some googly eyes.

ROCKET!

ZOOM! UP, UP AND AWAY I GO, I AM A ROCKET DON'T YOU KNOW? JUST **LOOK AT ME GO** AS I SOAR THROUGH SPACE. THERE'S **NO** WAY THAT I HAVE BEEN MADE FROM **TISSUE PAPER AND PAINTS!**

YOU WILL NEED

- ONE TOILET ROLL
- COLOURED PAINT
- COLOURED CARD
- SAFETY SCISSORS
- TAPE AND GLUE
- TIN FOIL
- TISSUE PAPER

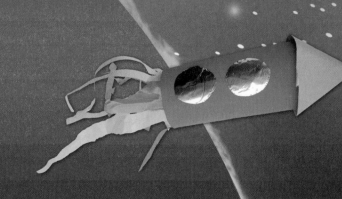

SET THE SCENE

Decorate a piece of black card with tin foil, silver stars and colourful planets for an out-of-this-world background. Paint planets, copy them from a book or cut pictures out of a magazine. Want to make your very own awesome rocket? Of course you do! Blast off to the next page to find out how…

DID YOU KNOW? HUMANS FIRST LANDED (AND WALKED!) ON THE MOON IN 1969.

I'M OFF TO VISIT THE MOON…

GO FURTHER!

IF YOU DON'T FANCY MAKING ROCKETS, YOU CAN TRY THESE FANTASTIC FAIRY HOUSES INSTEAD. TURN OVER AND WE'LL SHOW YOU JUST WHAT TO DO.

I'M A ROCKET!

1 Paint your toilet roll all over in any colour you like (we've gone for rocket red!). Leave to dry.

2 Make a circle by drawing around a large roll of tape or a cereal bowl and cut it out. Snip out a large triangle, like above, and roll it into a cone shape. Use some sticky tape to keep it in place.

3 Tape the cone in place on top of the rocket, then stick on some tin foil circles to make portholes.

4 Tear fire-coloured tissue paper into strips.

Tape the shredded tissue paper to the inside of the rocket at the bottom.

5

Now you know how, you can make lots of different colourful rockets! Get creative by decorating them in fun ways.

6

I AM NOT A TOILET ROLL...

I'M A FAIRY HOUSE!

Making fairy houses from toilet rolls is almost the same as making rockets. This time, when you make your paper cone, cut to give it a zigzag edge. Next snip in a little door for your fairies to come and go as they please, and make windows from paper or paint them on, it's up to you!

PiRATE!

HELLO THERE, MATEY! I BE A PIRATE AND I'VE **SAILED THE SEVEN SEAS** ON MY SHIP IN SEARCH OF **TREASURE**. ANYONE WHO SAYS I'M A TOILET ROLL CAN **WALK THE PLANK!**

YOU WILL NEED

- ONE EMPTY TOILET ROLL
- PAINTS AND BRUSHES
- WHITE PAPER
- SAFETY SCISSORS
- GLUE
- BLACK CARD
- BLACK PEN
- OPTIONAL: TISSUE PAPER

SET THE SCENE

Make an island scene for your pirate ship with a sheet of blue paper for the sea and a yellow paper desert island stuck on top. Now you're ready for treasure hunting. X marks the spot! Ready to make your pirate pal? Turn over to find out how.

ARRR, ME HEARTIES!

DID YOU KNOW?

LOTS OF PIRATE SHIPS HAVE A FLAG WITH A SKULL AND CROSSBONES ON IT. THIS IS CALLED THE JOLLY ROGER.

GO FURTHER!

MAKE A TOILET ROLL TREASURE CHEST FOR YOUR PIRATES TO KEEP THEIR PRECIOUS TREASURE! TURN OVER TO FOLLOW OUR SIMPLE STEP-BY-STEP GUIDE.

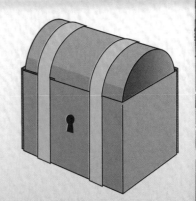

I'M A PIRATE!

1

Paint half of your toilet roll in a skin colour of your choice and then leave it to dry.

2

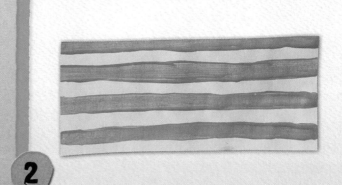

To make a striped top, cut a strip of paper (16cm x 5cm). Now paint or draw some stripes.

3

Stick your top on your pirate, then paint the bottom of the toilet roll black for the trousers.

4

Cut a pirate hat shape out of black card. Then cut out a skull and cross from white paper and stick them onto the hat.

5

Tape your hat to the top of your toilet roll. Draw your pirate's face with a black pen and add an eye patch for the finishing touch. Arrr, me hearties! Ready to set sail!

6

If you prefer, you could make a bandana for your pirate buddy! Just wrap tissue paper around your pirate's head and make a little knot shape to one side.

I AM NOT A TOILET ROLL...
I'M A TREASURE CHEST!

First, cut a toilet roll in half widthways to make the curved lid of the chest. Then cut a toilet roll in half lengthways and flatten out the card. Then make folds in the flattened-out card to tape it into a box. Next pop the lid inside and paint to decorate your chest.

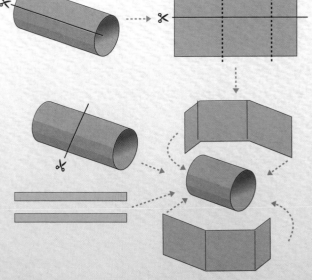

UNICORN!

NO, YOU'RE NOT DREAMING, I AM A MAGICAL UNICORN, AND I'M HERE TO MAKE FRIENDS WITH YOU! GRANTING WISHES AND MAKING YOUR DREAMS COME TRUE IS ALL I'VE EVER WANTED TO DO.

YOU WILL NEED

- ONE EMPTY TOILET ROLL
- WHITE, PINK AND BLACK PAINT
- SAFETY SCISSORS
- COLOURFUL TISSUE PAPER
- WHITE AND PINK CARD
- GLUE AND TAPE
- GLITTER
- RAINBOW TISSUE PAPER
- GOOGLY EYES

JOIN MY UNICORN SQUAD!

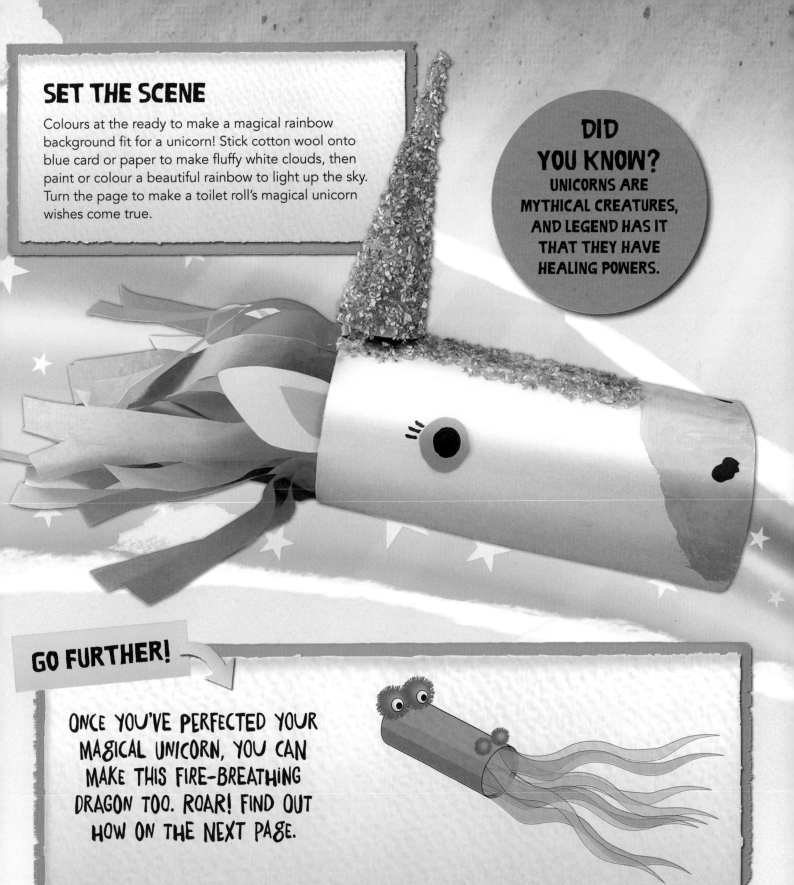

SET THE SCENE

Colours at the ready to make a magical rainbow background fit for a unicorn! Stick cotton wool onto blue card or paper to make fluffy white clouds, then paint or colour a beautiful rainbow to light up the sky. Turn the page to make a toilet roll's magical unicorn wishes come true.

DID YOU KNOW?
UNICORNS ARE MYTHICAL CREATURES, AND LEGEND HAS IT THAT THEY HAVE HEALING POWERS.

GO FURTHER!

ONCE YOU'VE PERFECTED YOUR MAGICAL UNICORN, YOU CAN MAKE THIS FIRE-BREATHING DRAGON TOO. ROAR! FIND OUT HOW ON THE NEXT PAGE.

I'M A UNICORN!

1

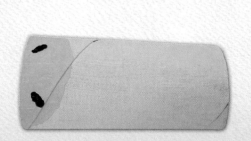

Paint your toilet roll white with a pink semi-circle at the end. When it is dry, dab on two black nostrils using the other end of a paintbrush.

2

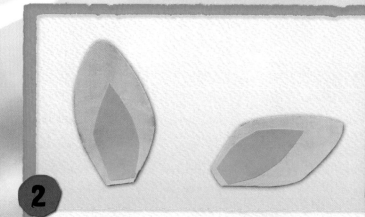

Carefully cut out two ear shapes from white card, then cut out smaller ear shapes in pink to make the insides of the ears. Glue them together.

3

To make the unicorn's horn, cut a triangle out of card, roll it into a cone shape and tape it in place. Next cover the cone in glue and sprinkle with gold glitter until it is completely covered.

4

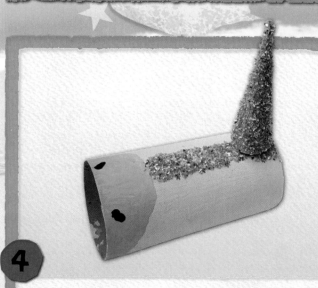

Carefully tape the horn onto the top of the unicorn. Then add a thick line of glue from the horn to the nose and sprinkle it with glitter.

5

To make the mane, cut out strips of rainbow coloured tissue paper and tape them to the end of the toilet roll by the horn.

6

Finally, tape the unicorn ears either side of its horn and add some googly eyes from the back of your book.

I AM NOT A TOILET ROLL...
I'M A DRAGON!

To make your amazing dragon, paint a toilet roll red or green and leave it to dry. For the eyes, stick two googly eyes onto pompoms and glue these onto the dragon. Now use two more pompoms for nostrils. Snip out strips of yellow and orange tissue paper to tape to the dragon's mouth. ROOAAARR!

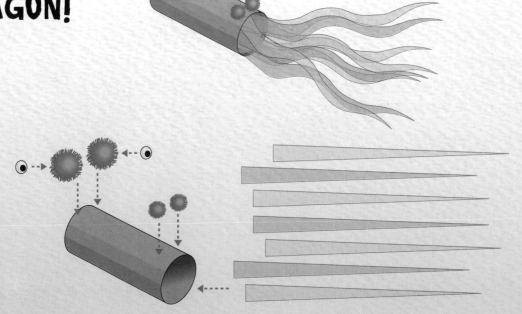

NINJAAAA!

WATCH ME ROLL WITH MY AWESOME NINJA SKILLS. I'M THE SPEEDIEST AND MOST POWERFUL NINJA AROUND SO THERE'S NO WAY THAT I AM A TOILET ROLL.

HI-YAH!

YOU WILL NEED

- ONE EMPTY TOILET ROLL
- DARK PAINT
- SAFE SCISSORS
- PINK PAPER
- BLACK PEN
- GLUE
- BLACK CARD
- STRING

SET THE SCENE

Cut out rectangles from tracing paper and stick them onto a sheet of black card to make a cool Dojo-style background. Want to give a toilet roll some nifty ninja moves? You can make your nimble ninja on the next page.

DID YOU KNOW?
NINJAS ORIGINALLY CAME FROM JAPAN AND WERE CALLED SHINOBI-NO-MONO.

I'M A MARTIAL ARTS MASTER!

GO FURTHER!

TAKE YOUR MAKE TO THE NEXT LEVEL BY CREATING A HORSE FOR YOUR NINJA TO RIDE. TURN OVER TO FIND OUT HOW.

I'M A NINJA!

1

Paint a toilet roll any colour you like (we recommend a dark colour) and leave it to dry.

2

Cut a small rectangle from pink paper and draw on some eyes. This will be your ninja's face.

3

Stick the face to the toilet roll, then carefully snip some small rectangles out of black card, and glue them over your ninja's eyes to make eyebrows.

4

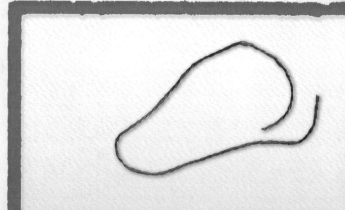

Next, cut out another thin rectangle from black card (10cm) and get your length of string ready.

5

Tie the string around the ninja's waist and slot the card stick inside, like this.

6

Now you can make a whole ninja crew using different colours. Sayonara for now!

I AM NOT A TOILET ROLL...
I'M A HORSE!

Tape two toilet rolls together, like this, to make the horse's head and body. Slot in a circle of card for the horse's nose and give it some nostrils with black paint. Cut out four legs from card and tape them in place ready to gallop. Make pointy paper ears and add two googly eyes. Wool makes a great mane and tail!

GINGERBREAD MAN!

HELLO THERE! I'M A **FRIENDLY GINGERBREAD MAN**, SWEET AS CAN BE. MY BUTTONS ARE MADE FROM DELICIOUS **CANDY**, NOT PAPER AND GLUE.

YOU WILL NEED

- ONE EMPTY TOILET ROLL
- ORANGE PAINT AND BRUSH
- SAFETY SCISSORS
- ORANGE CARD
- STICKY TAPE
- COLOURFUL PAPER
- GLUE

SET THE SCENE

Make a cunning fox out of orange and brown paper to help the gingerbread man get across a river of torn blue paper. But watch out for the fox's tricks! Ready to make your toilet roll gingerbread man? Turn over to find out how.

DID YOU KNOW?
THE BIGGEST GINGERBREAD HOUSE EVER WAS 21 FT TALL AND MADE IN TEXAS!

I LOVE MY FANCY BOW TIE!

GO FURTHER!

YOU COULD MAKE A SUPER COOL CLOWN USING THIS TECHNIQUE! FIND OUT HOW OVER ON THE NEXT PAGE.

I'M A GINGERBREAD MAN!

1

Paint a toilet roll all over with orange or yellow paint and leave it to one side to dry.

2

Next, cut a balloon shape (as above) out of orange card. Use coloured paper or marker pens to create your gingerbread man's face.

3

Tape the head to the top of the toilet roll.

4

Now, carefully cut two strips of orange card (15cm x 3cm) for the legs, and two strips (15cm x 2cm) for the arms.

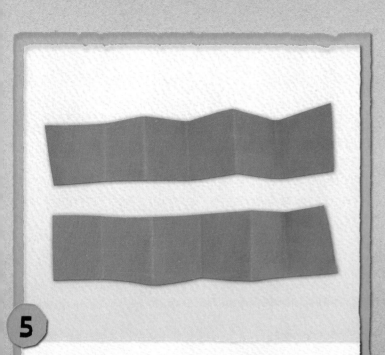

5 Fold the strips of card like this, to make them springy. Then use tape to attach the arms and legs to the body.

6 Decorate your new gingerbread buddy by sticking on colourful paper buttons and a bright bow tie.

7 Make a simple candy cane by cutting out this shape from card and painting on some bright red stripes.

I AM NOT A TOILET ROLL...
I'M A CLOWN!

Paint your toilet roll and then add your colourful bow tie and buttons. This time, you'll need white card for the face! Draw on some black crosses for the eyes, and then add a red smiley mouth and round nose. Snip out arms and big feet from card to tape in place and use wool to make hair.

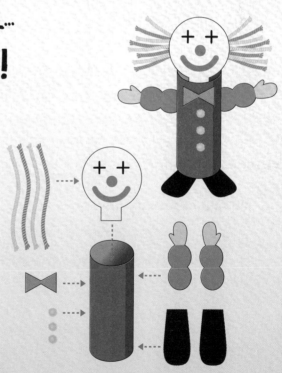

CASTLE!

I'M A **BEAUTIFUL** CASTLE! HOME TO THE **FINEST ROYALTY.** WITH MY TALL TOWERS TOPPED WITH **FABULOUS FLAGS,** I'M FAR TOO **GRAND** TO BE MADE FROM CARDBOARD!

YOU WILL NEED

- THREE EMPTY TOILET ROLLS
- SAFE SCISSORS
- PAINTS AND BRUSHES
- PAPER
- GLUE
- LOLLIPOP STICKS OR TOOTHPICKS
- BLUE AND BROWN PAPER
- BLACK PEN
- TAPE

SET THE SCENE

Pop your castle onto layers of green paper to make rolling countryside. Add trees like these shown or scrunch up tissue paper for colourful flowers.
Turn over to find out how to transform three toilet rolls into a splendid castle fit for a king and queen.

DID YOU KNOW?
MOATS PROTECT CASTLES AND KEEP OUT ANY UNWELCOME VISITORS.

GO FURTHER!

WHY STOP AT JUST THREE CASTLE TOWERS? LET'S MAKE YOUR CASTLE EVEN MORE SPECTACULAR! WE WILL SHOW YOU HOW ON THE NEXT PAGE.

I'M A CASTLE!

1

Cut rectangles from the top of your toilet roll to create turrets.

2

Repeat Step 1 on two more toilet rolls. You could make some towers shorter by trimming the tops off first.

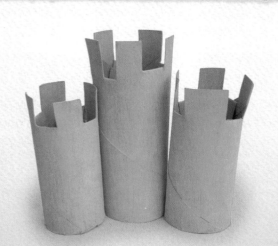

3

Paint all the toilet rolls in your favourite colour and leave them to one side to dry.

4

To make flags, cut triangles out of colourful paper and tape them to lollipop sticks or wooden toothpicks. When your castle is dry, tape the flags to the top of your towers.

5

Cut three windows out of blue paper, and one door out of brown paper or card.

6

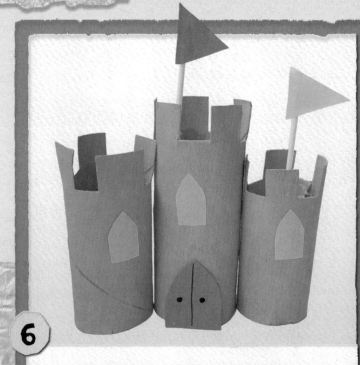

Next, tape all three towers together, before sticking on your windows and door.

I AM NOT A TOILET ROLL...
I'M A HUGE CASTLE!

You don't have to stop at just three toilet rolls. Keep taping on more and more painted toilet roll towers until you make a super grand castle! You could stick all of your towers onto a painted cardboard box, like this. Have fun designing lots of different door and window shapes as you go.

MERMAID!

PERCHED ON A ROCK NEAR THE SEA SHORE, I SIT AND SING MY MERRY MERMAID SONGS IN THE SUN. WITH MY SHIMMERING TAIL AND LONG HAIR, EVERYONE KNOWS WHO I AM!

TRA LA LA LAAAAAA!

YOU WILL NEED

- ONE TOILET ROLL
- PAINTS AND BRUSHES
- SAFETY SCISSORS
- COLOURFUL PAPER
- CARD
- GLUE AND TAPE
- PEN

SET THE SCENE

Scrunch up brown paper bags to make a rock for your mermaid to sit on. If you visit the seaside, you could even bring back some pebbles for a rockpool scene. Ready to make your mermaid? Swim over the page to find out how.

Swim over the page to find out how.

DID YOU KNOW?
A MALE VERSION OF A MERMAID IS CALLED A MERMAN.

GO FURTHER!

DO YOU WANT TO MAKE SOME COLOURFUL CORAL REEFS FOR YOUR MERMAID TO SWIM AROUND AND EXPLORE? WE WILL SHOW YOU HOW ON THE NEXT PAGE.

I'M A MERMAID!

1 Paint the top half of your toilet roll in a skin colour of your choice and the bottom half in a nice, bright colour. Leave them to dry.

2 Carefully cut a mermaid tail from some card. Paint this card to match the colour of the tail part of your toilet roll and leave it to dry.

3 For the hair, cut out strips of colourful paper and roll the ends of each strip around a pencil to make it curl.

4 Now tape each piece of hair to the top of the toilet roll. We stuck on a paper fringe, too!

5

Make a shell bikini from colourful paper and use a black pen to draw on some detail. Now glue the shells in place and draw on a smiley face.

6

Tape the tail to the back of your mermaid. Now she is ready for any underwater adventure!

I AM NOT A TOILET ROLL...
I'M A CORAL REEF!

Paint a toilet roll turquoise and when it's dry, stick on strips of colourful paper and tissue to look like coral or seaweed. Then make your own tropical sea creatures and hide them in the bits of coral or seaweed, too. You can make lots of corals in different colours!

YOUR DESIGNS

NOW IT'S OVER TO YOU... THE ONLY THING HOLDING YOUR EMPTY TOILET ROLLS BACK FROM GREATNESS IS YOUR OWN IMAGINATION! SKETCH YOUR IDEAS HERE — WE'VE GIVEN YOU A COUPLE OF ROLLS TO GET YOU STARTED.

. . . .

shark fins

shark fins

bat wings

googly eyes

castle door

unicorn ear

unicorn horn

unicorn ear

mermaid's tail

pirate hat

candy cane